YOU CHOOSE
BOOKS ™

The
Wild West

An Interactive History Adventure

by Allison Lassieur

Consultant:
Malcolm Rohrbough, Professor of History
University of Iowa
Author, *Days of Gold: The California Gold Rush
and the American Nation*

Capstone
press ®

Mankato, Minnesota

You Choose Books are published by Capstone Press,
151 Good Counsel Drive, P.O. Box 669, Mankato, Minnesota 56002.
www.capstonepress.com

Printed in the United States of America in Stevens Point, Wisconsin
012010
005668R

Library of Congress Cataloging-in-Publication Data
Lassieur, Allison.
      The Wild West : an interactive history adventure / by Allison Lassieur.
      p. cm. — (You choose books)
      Includes bibliographical references and index.
      Summary: "Describes the people and events of the age of the Wild West in the year 1876. The reader's choices reveal the
historical details from the perspective of an outlaw, a lawman, and a fortune-seeker in Deadwood, Dakota Territory" — Provided
by publisher.
      ISBN-13: 978-1-4296-2342-1 (hardcover)   ISBN-13: 978-1-4296-3456-4 (softcover pbk.)
      ISBN-10: 1-4296-2342-X (hardcover)   ISBN-10: 1-4296-3456-1 (softcover pbk.)
      1. West (U.S.) — History — 19th century — Juvenile literature. 2. West (U.S.) — Biography — Juvenile literature. 3.
Frontier and pioneer life — West (U.S.) — Juvenile literature. 4. Outlaws — West (U.S.) — History — 19th century — Juvenile
literature. 5. Peace officers — West (U.S.) — History — 19th century — Juvenile literature. 6. Pioneers — West (U.S.) — History
— 19th century — Juvenile literature. I. Title. II. Series.
F596.L365 2009
978'.02 — dc22
                                                                                                    2008029841

Editorial Credits
Jennifer Besel, editor; Juliette Peters, set designer; Gene Bentdahl, book designer; Wanda Winch, photo researcher

Photo Credits
Adams Museum, Deadwood, SD, 74, 95
Butler Center for Arkansas Studies, Central Arkansas Library System, Little Rock, 52
Corbis/Bettmann, 10
The Denver Public Library, Western History/Genealogy Department, 81, 84
Fort Smith National Historic Site/NPS, 51, 64, 69
Getty Images Inc./Hulton Archive/American Stock, 77
Kansas State Historical Society, 47, 55
Library of Congress, Prints & Photographs Division, Civil War Photographs, [LC-USZ62-99872], 42;
      John C.H. Grabill Collection [LOT 3076-21, no. 3844], 93
Minnesota Historical Society/Sumner Studio, 17
Northfield Historical Society, 26
North Wind Picture Archives, 21, 100
Printroom.com Photography, 15, 25, 70
Triangle C Ranch Antiques and Collectibles, cover, 19, 33, 37, 87, 89, 103, 105
Wichita Public Library, Local History Section, Wichita, Kansas, 6
Wichita-Sedgwick County Historical Museum, 59

TABLE OF CONTENTS

ABOUT YOUR ADVENTURE

YOU are living in a small town in 1876. You've read about outlaws robbing banks and people mining for gold in the Wild West. You long for an exciting life too. You head west in search of adventure. Will you survive?

In this book, you'll explore how the choices people made meant the difference between life and death. The events you'll experience happened to real people.

Chapter One sets the scene. Then you choose which path to read. Follow the directions at the bottom of each page. The choices you make will change your outcome. After you finish one path, go back and read the others for new perspectives and more adventures.

YOU CHOOSE the path
you take through history.

White people heard wild stories of American Indians who lived in the vast wilderness of the West.

The Wild, Wild West

For most Americans in 1876, the land west of the Mississippi River is a strange and dangerous place. They've heard of outlaws who carry guns and aren't afraid to use them. Lawmen struggle to keep the peace. Citizens who have moved west just try to stay out of all the trouble.

Only a few years ago, the West was a vast wilderness that few white people had ever seen. Explorers and fur trappers who ventured west brought back amazing stories. They told of American Indian tribes and enormous herds of buffalo. They described a countryside so wild and fierce that people found the stories hard to believe.

Turn the page.

In 1848, everything changed. Gold was discovered in California, and the country was swept up in gold fever. Thousands of people traveled west with the hope of striking it rich.

But from 1861 to 1865, the Civil War tore apart the United States. The North and South fought over many differences. The biggest difference was whether slavery should be allowed. The fighting took attention away from the West for awhile.

After the war, soldiers found their old lives destroyed. They poured west in search of new lives. Former slaves also went west. In areas like Colorado and the Dakota Territory, silver and gold were discovered. Crowded towns sprang up almost overnight.

You've heard the stories of outlaws and the lawmen who hunt them. To you, the Wild West isn't frightening. It's a place of thrilling adventure.

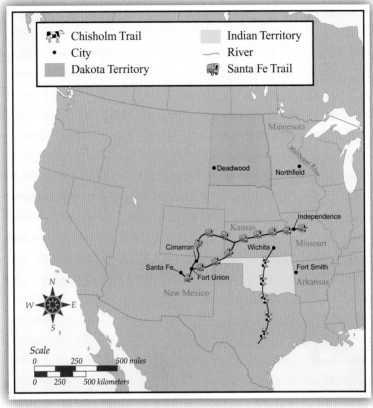

Chisholm Trail
City
Dakota Territory
Indian Territory
River
Santa Fe Trail

Minnesota

Mississippi River

• Deadwood
Northfield

Kansas
Independence

Cimarron
Wichita
Missouri

Santa Fe
Fort Union
Fort Smith

New Mexico
Arkansas

N
W   E
S

Scale
0   250   500 miles
0   250   500 kilometers

❧ To explore the West as an outlaw, turn to page 11.

❧ To find adventure as a lawman, turn to page 43.

❧ To seek your fortune in Deadwood in Dakota Territory,
turn to page 71.

THE JAMES BOYS WEEKLY.

Containing Stories of Adventure.

Issued Weekly—By Subscription $2.50 per year. Entered as Second Class Matter at the New York Post Office, by Frank Tousey.

No. 1.   NEW YORK, DECEMBER 28, 1900.   Price 5 Cent

THE JAMES BOYS
-OR-
THE BANDIT KING'S LAST SHOT.
BY D. W. STEVENS.

OVERLAND STAGE.

U.S. MAIL

U.S. MAIL

$ MAIL.

Even after the days of the Wild West, books called dime novels spread tales of outlaws robbing the rich.

CHAPTER 2

Running from the Law

Life on a small Missouri farm is all you've ever known. Before the Civil War, things were pretty good. But in 1861, Father marched to war and never came home. The war ended in 1865, when you were 10. Now it's early 1876. Deep inside, you feel a longing and a restlessness you can't explain. The only thing that excites you are the stories of the wild outlaws of the West.

Turn the page.

One day, you have had enough. You're 21 years old, plenty old enough to leave the farm. You pack your bags and take your guns. Then you kiss your mother good-bye, promise to write, and set off on horseback. You're not sure where you're going. Wherever you go, you'll be looking for excitement and maybe some gold.

You've heard tales of lone gunslingers robbing stagecoaches in the far West. Maybe you could head to New Mexico Territory on the Santa Fe Trail. You've also heard about gangs of outlaws robbing banks in towns on the prairie. You think over your options as you ride through the countryside.

→ To travel farther west on the Santa Fe Trail,
go to page 13.

→ To look for adventure on the prairie,
turn to page 16.

You think you'll have a better chance of stealing gold if you head farther west. There are fewer lawmen there to get in the way. You head to Independence, Missouri, and join a wagon train going west on the Santa Fe Trail. It's a long, hard journey. Finally you get to Fort Union in New Mexico. You decide now is a good time to go out on your own.

You don't know much about New Mexico Territory. You walk up to a soldier. "Are there any towns nearby?" you ask him.

"There's a town about 90 miles north of here called Cimarron," he tells you. "But it's a wild place. Just last year they had a huge fight over land ownership, called the Colfax County War. Lots of men died in gunfights and such."

Turn the page.

That sounds like the perfect town for you. A few days later you're riding down the main street of Cimarron. It's larger than you expected. You stop a stranger on the street.

"Is there a hotel or restaurant in town?" you ask.

"Well, there's the Lambert Inn," the man says, pointing at a large building. "Be careful if you go there. Every morning we all wonder who was killed at Lambert's last night."

"Thank you," you say as the man walks away. At the inn, you order lunch and notice that the ceiling is filled with bullet holes. Three dusty strangers are talking at a table beside you.

The Lambert Inn was a bar, restaurant, and hotel. Many outlaws stayed there while traveling through town.

"Yeah, it's true," one says. "The stagecoach arrives at noon Friday, and it's carrying a box of gold. They're taking it to the bank."

You would be rich if you could get your hands on that box. But how will you do it?

⇢ To rob the stagecoach, turn to page **20**.

⇢ To rob the bank after the gold is brought there, turn to page **23**.

For weeks, you ride through the open country. Everywhere you go, you hear stories about the great Jesse James and his gang. You would love to ride with a gang like that. Every once in a while, you read a letter from Jesse James in a newspaper. He always denies the crimes he is rumored to have committed.

By the summer of 1876, you find yourself in St. Paul, Minnesota. The big news is that the James gang just robbed the Missouri Pacific railroad train in Missouri.

William Stiles was also known as Bill Chadwell. No one is sure which was his real name.

One afternoon, you go to a general store. To your shock, you see a familiar face! It's William Stiles, a friend that you met in Missouri. You have heard that he is friendly with Jesse James, but you're not sure you believe it. You spend some time catching up. Then the talk comes around to the James gang.

"I'd love to ride with the gang," you say.

Stiles looks hard at you. Then he says, "Meet me in the saloon later."

Turn the page.

When you arrive at the saloon, Stiles is sitting at a dim corner table with two strangers. "This is Jesse and Frank James," Stiles says in a hushed voice. He turns to Jesse. "This one is OK. I know him. We can trust him."

Jesse looks at you. "If Stiles here says you're OK, that's good enough for me. We're robbing the bank in Northfield."

Jesse lays out the plan. The gang members will travel separately down to Northfield. Before the raid, they'll meet outside of town. Then they'll divide into three groups. One group will go into the bank and rob it. The second group will serve as lookouts on the street in front of the bank. The third group will guard the getaway road at the edge of town.

"You can join the lookout group. Or you can go into the bank with Frank," Jesse says.

Brothers Jesse James (left) and Frank James (right) often planned and committed robberies together.

→ To join the lookout group, turn to page 25.

→ To help rob the bank, turn to page 27.

You figure it'll be easier to rob the stage before it gets to town. But you need to make sure there's going to be gold on that stagecoach. And if there's gold, who's guarding it? The next morning, you head to the Barlow, Sanderson, and Company Stage office to gather some information.

"When does the stage arrive?" you ask the man behind the counter. "My sister is coming out for a visit." You think your lie sounds pretty good.

"Friday at noon," the man replies.

You nod. "How safe is that stage, anyway?" you ask. "I hear that Indians sometimes attack the stages."

"Oh, this one is safe enough," the man says. "There's a shotgun messenger on the stage, and he's a good shot."

Drivers and messengers were armed to protect passengers and money on the stages.

"Surely the driver is armed too," you say.

"Most of them are," the man says. "Driving a stage can be dangerous work."

"Thanks," you say as you leave. A shotgun messenger! They are paid to guard large sums of money on a stagecoach. Now you are sure there will be gold on the stage.

Turn the page.

Friday arrives. You and your horse hide behind a boulder near the road outside town. Finally you hear the rumble of wheels on gravel. The large stagecoach rounds the bend. Two men ride on the high front seat.

You draw your guns and gallop to the stagecoach. "Stop the stage now!" you yell.

As the stage slows, the shotgun messenger stands up and fires at you, but his shot misses. You shoot, hitting the man in the leg. He falls to the ground, bleeding.

"Don't shoot no more!" the driver yells, raising his hands. "I'm unarmed!"

That's odd, you think. The man at the stagecoach office said drivers usually have guns.

→ If you trust the stagecoach driver, turn to page **30**.

→ If you think the driver is lying, turn to page **31**.

It's risky for a lone robber to hold up a stagecoach. But an individual can easily get into a bank, you think.

You watch the bank for the next three days. The bank is a small but elegant stone building with columns along the front. You discover that every afternoon at 1:00 almost everyone at the bank leaves for lunch. One teller stays on duty. A door at the back of the bank will work for a getaway.

On Friday, you wait for the stagecoach to arrive. When it does, the driver carries a large box into the bank. The bank manager and the shotgun messenger guard it. When they leave for lunch, you casually walk inside.

Turn the page.

"Excuse me," you say politely to the teller. "Can you make change for this bill, please?" You hand the teller a $20 bill.

"Of course, sir," the small man replies. When he opens the cash box, you whip out your guns and point them at the man's head.

"And get me the rest of the money out of the safe while you're at it," you say. "I want that lockbox."

The man's eyes are wide with terror. "I can't do that," he says. "I don't have the key to the safe."

➤ If you believe the man, turn to page 32.

➤ If you think the teller is lying, turn to page 35.

The James brothers often rode with the Younger brothers, robbing banks and trains.

On the morning of September 7, you meet the gang outside the town of Northfield. Stiles introduces you to Cole Younger and Clell Miller, the other guys in the lookout group. You also meet the other gang members, Bob and Jim Younger and Charlie Pitts.

Your heart is pounding. You, Frank, Bob, and Charlie arrive in town first. A few minutes later, the rest of the gang arrives. Frank, Bob, and Charlie head inside the bank. You, Cole, and Clell stay out front. The other guys head to the end of the street.

Turn the page.

The bank's counters were very low, so they were easy to jump over.

A man tries to follow Frank into the bank. Clell pulls out his gun and grabs the man.

"Stand back!" Clell yells.

The man jerks out of Clell's grasp and runs down the street, yelling, "Get your guns, boys. They're robbing the bank!" People start screaming and running for cover. Then you hear gunfire from inside the bank. You quickly realize this situation has gone very wrong.

➻ To run for your life, turn to page 33.

➻ To draw your gun to defend yourself, turn to page 34.

You want to be inside that bank. On the morning of September 7, Stiles takes you to meet the gang outside Northfield. There's Jesse and Frank. Three brothers named Cole, Bob, and Jim Younger are there too. You also meet Charlie Pitts and Clell Miller.

You, Frank, Bob, and Charlie arrive in town together and go to Lee and Hitchcock's general store. You sit around casually, trying not to draw attention to yourselves. A little while later, the rest of the gang rides into town. Jesse, Stiles, and Jim ride slowly to the end of the street. Cole and Clell stay outside the bank. Then you, Charlie, Bob, and Frank enter the bank.

Turn the page.

Three men are working inside the bank. No one takes notice as you enter. Then one man looks up. You draw your gun and grin. The man's eyes fly open in shock.

"Put your hands up!" you say, jumping over the counter. "We're going to rob this bank!"

"Don't any of you holler," Charlie says. "We've got 40 men outside."

Frank waves his pistol at one of the men. "Are you the teller?" he demands.

"No," the man says. Frank asks the other two men the same question. Both of them also say no.

Frank points his gun at one man and says, "Open that safe, quick, or I'll blow your head off."

"It can't be opened," the man says. "It's got a time lock. It'll only open at a certain time of day."

One of the bank employees begins shouting, "Murder! Murder!" You hit him with the butt of your gun. He falls to the floor. The other two men continue to refuse to open the safe. Panic rises in your chest. It isn't supposed to happen this way!

Suddenly you hear gunfire and shouting outside. It grows louder, as if a crowd is headed toward the bank. One of the employees bolts for the back door. Charlie shoots at him, but the man gets away. At that moment you hear one of your partners outside yell, "The game is up! Better get out, boys. They're killing all our men!"

→ *If you go out the front, turn to page* **33**.

→ *To try to escape out the back, turn to page* **36**.

You lower your guns. Immediately the driver reaches under the seat and pulls out a rifle. You fire at him, but your horse rears and you miss. The blast from the driver misses you. You dig your heels into your horse and flee, bending low over the horse's neck to avoid the gunfire.

Another rifle blast misses you. But a shot from the downed shotgun messenger doesn't. You fall off your horse, landing in a pool of your own blood. Your outlaw days are over before they began.

THE END

To follow another path, turn to page 9.
To read the conclusion, turn to page 101.

You know better than to trust the driver. "Get off the coach!" you yell, pointing your guns at him. Quickly you tie his hands together. You climb up to the seat and find the lockbox. You haul it down and tie it to your saddle.

But there's more loot to be had. Three passengers are inside the stagecoach — a boy, an old woman, and a Chinese man.

"Empty your pockets!" you growl.

Soon you have a fistful of money, diamond earrings, and a gold pocket watch. As you turn toward your horse, a gunshot rings through the air.

→ To jump on your horse and try to escape, turn to page **39**.

→ If you turn and fight, turn to page **40**.

You didn't plan for this. You start to panic. "OK, give me everything you have right there," you say. The man stuffs a wad of bills and a handful of coins into a bag. You grab the bag from him.

"Now get on the floor with your head down," you say, "and you won't get hurt." The man obeys. Quickly you dash down the hall to the back door. As you do, you can hear the man run out the front shouting, "The bank has been robbed!"

Cursing, you run out the door and jump on your horse. You gallop down the street as shouts and yells echo behind you. You aren't even out of town before a large posse of angry men thunders behind you.

➻ If you give up, turn to page 37.

➻ If you try to get away, turn to page 38.

32

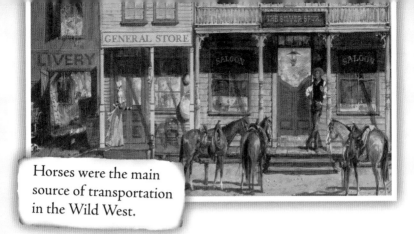

Horses were the main source of transportation in the Wild West.

You rush straight for your horse. As you untie the horse, you duck to avoid gunfire from the townspeople. Then you jump into the saddle and wheel your horse around. You race for the back of the bank, hoping no one will shoot you. Miraculously, you make it. You race wildly out of town, not looking back. Life in an outlaw gang is not for you. Maybe it's time to go back to the farm. It might be dull, but at least no one shoots at you.

33

THE END

To follow another path, turn to page 9.
To read the conclusion, turn to page 101.

You, Clell, and Cole spring onto your horses and pull out your guns. Jesse and the other gang members guarding the road gallop into town, cursing and shooting. The air is filled with gunfire, shouting, and the crashing of glass. Suddenly gunfire comes from the buildings. Finally Frank, Bob, and Charlie come out of the bank. You yell at the townspeople to get inside the buildings. But they keep shooting at all of you. Jim is shot in the face, and Frank is hit in the leg.

You need to get out of here. As you ride furiously out of town, you feel a burning pain rip through your side. For a moment, you stay on your galloping horse as your warm blood flows out of the wound. Then you slip to the ground. You die alone in the dust.

THE END

To follow another path, turn to page 9.
To read the conclusion, turn to page 101.

"You're lying," you say, cocking back the hammer on your gun. The man swallows hard. He hands over a shiny brass key. "This better be the right key, or you'll regret it," you say.

It is the right key. Inside the safe are stacks of bills and piles of gold coins. You stuff your pockets with the money. Quickly you head out the back door and mount your horse.

You trot slowly down the street. You turn a corner and then gallop like mad out of town. No one seems to know what has happened. You smile and pat your bulging pockets. You're going to be a hunted man, but you don't care. You don't even stop to wonder about whose money you just stole. All you know is that you've made the choice to live as an outlaw.

THE END

To follow another path, turn to page 9.
To read the conclusion, turn to page 101.

Rushing out the back, you fire your guns at anything moving. A rock hits you in the back. The townspeople are throwing rocks at you! You duck down an alley. You see Frank on his horse. He's bleeding. You jump onto the back of his horse and gallop out of town.

A few miles outside of town you meet up with what is left of the gang.

"Who's here?" you ask breathlessly.

Jesse replies, "Everyone but Clell and Stiles. They were killed."

Everyone is bleeding. Fear and panic grip you as you gallop madly away. The gang only got $26 and some change from this mess. And now you're an outlaw on the run.

THE END

To follow another path, turn to page 9.
To read the conclusion, turn to page 101.

Hanging was a common punishment for criminals in the Wild West.

You stop. "I surrender!" you shout.

The posse surrounds you. They take you directly to the jail.

After a quick trial, your hanging is set for the next day. You realize that you are going to die. You're led to the gallows. You stand as the noose is tightened around your throat. As the hangman pulls the lever, your outlaw days end.

THE END

To follow another path, turn to page 9.
To read the conclusion, turn to page 101.

If they catch you, they'll kill you. Desperately you urge your horse forward. You're in such a panic that you drop the bag of money. You don't get too much farther when the posse catches up to you. You raise your hands and drop your weapons. The posse surrounds you, several guns aimed at your heart.

"Where's the money?" one man shouts at you.

"What money?" you say in your most innocent voice. "I don't have any money!"

"You're a liar and a thief," a greasy man growls. "I saw you rob the bank." A blast from his shotgun is the last thing you hear as you die.

THE END

To follow another path, turn to page 9.
To read the conclusion, turn to page 101.

You don't wait to see where the shot came from. Jumping on your horse, you race away. A final gunshot zings past your ear but misses.

You ride hard for several miles. By then you're certain no one is following you — for now. Dropping to the ground, you quickly break the lock on the box. Your heart leaps when you see piles of cash, stacks of coins, and bags full of gold nuggets. Quickly you stuff everything into your saddlebag and throw the box down a gully.

As you get back on your horse, you realize you'll be hunted and chased wherever you go. Strangely, though, the thought doesn't frighten you. You're not sure where you'll go next, but it really doesn't matter. You're a real outlaw now.

THE END

To follow another path, turn to page 9.
To read the conclusion, turn to page 101.

You turn and see the wounded shotgun messenger on his feet, pointing his gun at you.

"Put down your weapon," you shout to the man. "I don't want to kill you, but I will if I have to!"

"Not if I kill you first!" the messenger says, firing his gun. A bullet slams into your left shoulder and you stagger backward. You fire, and the bullet hits the man in the chest. He falls to the ground in a puff of dust.

You climb onto your horse and ride away. You begin to feel dizzy and thirsty. Looking down, you're shocked to see that you are covered in blood.

"Guess I got hit bad," you say to yourself as you slide off the horse's back. You find a patch of shade under a cactus and lie down. The desert sand is stained red with your blood. You can't see the lockbox that you tied to your saddle.

As you fade into unconsciousness, you realize that the lockbox must have fallen off when you raced away from the stagecoach. "All that for nothing," you think, as your life bleeds away.

THE END

To follow another path, turn to page 9.
To read the conclusion, turn to page 101.

Many Civil War soldiers headed west after the war, looking for a new life.

CHAPTER 3

Keeping the Peace

You grew up on a farm in Ohio. When the Civil War started in 1861, you joined the Union army. Your skill with a gun got you a position as a sharpshooter. After the war, you returned to your family's small, sleepy farm. Not much happens here, and you long for some excitement.

You've heard stories about the lawless towns of the West, where thieves and murderers run wild. Colorful tales fill newspapers and cheap novels. But instead of being excited by their adventures, you are disgusted. You think outlaws should pay for their crimes.

Turn the page.

It's now 1876, and you have caught what people call western fever. All you can think about is going west and finding work as a lawman. But you're not sure how to go about it. The answer comes one afternoon as you're buying supplies at the general store in town.

"Did you hear the news?" your friend Henry asks you. "A new federal judge was appointed to slow the crime in Indian Territory. His court is in Fort Smith, Arkansas."

"What's his name?" you ask, curious.

"Isaac Parker. He used to be a U.S. congressman. And he's looking to hire some deputy marshals."

Your heart leaps with excitement. "Are you going out there?" you ask.

"Nope," Henry replies. "I'm headed to Wichita, Kansas. I hear there are jobs there. A man can work as a cowboy with one of the big cattle drives. You know, they could probably use some deputy sheriffs in Wichita. Wichita is a rough town. Those rowdy cowboys sure cause trouble. I think Wyatt Earp is the law there now. He's one of the most fearless lawmen I've ever seen."

Lawmen are needed, and you would make a great one. But where do you go?

❖ To go to Wichita with Henry, turn to page **46**.

❖ To head to Arkansas, turn to page **50**.

The next week, you and Henry board a train for Wichita. When you arrive, you can't believe what you see. At least 100 wagons clatter through the muddy streets. The air vibrates with the bellowing of thousands of cattle.

Henry claps you on the back. "Just a few years ago, this town was nothin' more than a speck on the prairie," he says. "Then the railroad came through. Cattlemen started driving their herds here to catch the trains east. This town is a big stop on the Chisholm Trail."

"Where do I find the marshal?" you ask.

"Try the jail," Henry replies. He shakes your hand good-bye. "Good luck to you."

Henry disappears into the crowd. You push through the crowds until you see the jailhouse. You push open the door and go inside.

Wichita, Kansas, was a booming cattle town by 1876.

"What can I do for you?" a tall man asks you. He's wearing a badge.

You introduce yourself. "I'm looking for a job," you say.

"I'm Mike Meagher," he says, shaking your hand. "I'm the city marshal."

You tell him about your sharpshooting experience in the Civil War. Meagher listens. He asks you a lot of questions.

Turn the page.

"I certainly need some help around here," he says when you're done. "You're in the right place at the right time."

"What happened to Wyatt Earp?" you ask. "I thought he was a lawman in Wichita."

"He was, until a while ago," Meagher replies. "He ran into some trouble around here earlier this year. Now I hear he's in Dodge City."

Meagher pins a small star to your coat. "You're an official deputy marshal of Wichita, Kansas."

As you're admiring your shiny badge, two men burst into the jailhouse. "There's some cowboys causing trouble down by the stock pens," one man says breathlessly.

"Lead the way," you tell him.

Down by the railroad tracks, thousands of cattle stand shoulder to shoulder in enormous crowded pens. The overwhelming smell makes your eyes water.

Five dirty cowboys are yelling and laughing near the edge of the stock pens. One of them draws his pistol and waves it drunkenly in the air.

You approach the group carefully, smiling and keeping your hands visible. One cowboy notices your badge. "So Meagher's got a shiny new deputy!"

Another cowboy spits onto the muddy ground. "We just came back from a long cattle drive. Our cheating trail boss hasn't paid us yet. We ain't going nowhere until we get paid."

→ To reason with the cowboys, turn to page **54**.

→ To arrest them, turn to page **62**.

When you arrive in Fort Smith, Arkansas, the town is buzzing with talk of the new judge.

"He condemned seven men to death in his first term of court!" one woman tells you in the general store.

A tall black man says, "Before Judge Parker came to town, Indian Territory was called Robber's Roost." He reaches out to shake your hand. "I'm George Winston, the bailiff in Judge Parker's courtroom." He nods to a white man beside him. "This here is James Fagan. He's the U.S. marshal in this area."

"I'd like to work as a deputy for Judge Parker," you say.

Fagan smiles. "You're in luck. I'm in charge of finding deputies for Judge Parker's court," he says. "Come with me."

Judge Parker became well known for his swift punishments of criminals.

Judge Parker is a demanding man with piercing eyes. You tell him about yourself.

"I like this one," Fagan says, clapping you on the back. "He'll do a good job for us."

"All right," the judge says. "Your job as deputy marshal is to search out criminals and return them to my court for justice. You'll be paid $2 for each arrest. You'll get six cents a mile going to the arrest and 10 cents a mile for yourself and each prisoner coming back."

Turn the page.

After being freed from slavery, Bass Reeves helped tame the Wild West.

A few days later, you're on the road with another deputy marshal, two guards, a cook, and a "grub" wagon. The other marshal is Bass Reeves. A former slave, he's now one of the most respected deputy marshals in the country.

Reeves lets you read the warrants that Judge Parker gave him. You're looking for a murderer and a horse thief.

"What will happen to these men when we catch them?" you ask.

"The judge will call witnesses and hear testimony. Sometimes the outlaw is hanged. Other times he goes to jail."

One afternoon, a man rides toward you. "You looking for that no-account murderer?" he asks. "That outlaw is staying with a family a few miles from here." He gives Reeves directions and then rides off.

"A lot of locals help criminals," Reeves says. "They'll give them food and hide them."

When you arrive at the farm, Reeves knocks on the farmhouse door. A tired-looking woman answers. "Can we speak to your husband?" he asks politely.

You look around. The farmer is nowhere to be seen. That's odd, you think. A farmer is usually outside working. Something isn't right.

→ To warn the others of your feeling, turn to page **56**.

→ To ignore your suspicions, turn to page **60**.

"This is a mighty big problem," you say. "You need to be paid. But I need you to get out of the stock pens. Tell you what. You come with me, and we'll find out where your pay is."

The men look at you suspiciously. "Well, he's the law, boys," one says. "If anyone can get that lying boss to pay us, it's him." The others nod in agreement. They put away their weapons and follow you out of the stock pens.

"Look — there's the trail boss!" one of them shouts.

"Wait, let me handle this," you say confidently. You rest your hand on the handle of your gun. Then you walk up to the man.

"These cowboys here claim that you owe them their pay," you say in a calm voice.

"I don't owe them lazy good-for-nothings anything!" the man says. "And I don't need no greenhorn lawman telling me what to do!" The man pulls his gun.

Herds of cattle were held in stock pens, waiting to be loaded onto eastbound trains.

❖ To draw your weapon, turn to page **58**.

❖ To try to disarm the man, turn to page **64**.

"I don't like this," you say in a low voice.

"Me, neither," says one of the guards. "It doesn't feel right."

"Let's separate and move back," you suggest. The others agree. You all slowly turn your horses around. One by one you separate and begin to leave. Suddenly you see a movement out of the corner of your eye. Someone is in the hayloft of the barn.

"Watch out, boys!" you cry, just as several bullets whiz past you. You jump from your horse and dash into the barn. One of the guards is hit. He's lying in a pool of blood.

Drawing your weapon, you inch forward through the dim barn. You can hear movement coming from above your head. Several more gun blasts shake the rafters. You've got to get up there and disarm the shooter, or others will die.

Slowly you climb the ladder to the hayloft. A figure is standing in the loft, his back to you. He hasn't seen you yet. Now is your chance to get him.

→ To try to shoot the man, turn to page **66**.

→ To try to sneak up on him, turn to page **67**.

You're ready for this. You draw your gun and fire at the man, aiming low. He howls and falls to the ground, clutching his leg as he drops his weapon. One of the cowboys reaches into the man's pocket and pulls out a wad of bills.

"This'll about do it!" he says. "Thank you, lawman!" The five cowboys dash away, laughing and whooping.

The man is still moaning and holding his leg, but you don't see any blood. "Are you hurt?" you ask. The man glares at you and lifts his hand. A tiny trickle of blood stains his trousers.

You laugh and help the man up. "Next time, pay the men what you owe them, and there won't be any trouble."

"I'll get you, lawman!" he shouts as he storms off.

Later you tell Meagher what happened. "I know that trail boss," he says. "He's always cheating the men out of their pay." Meagher smiles. "You'll do just fine here." You grin. You're going to like being a lawman in the Wild West.

Mike Meagher served as city marshal in Wichita, Kansas.

THE END

To follow another path, turn to page 9.
To read the conclusion, turn to page 101.

It's nothing, you think. Reeves tips his hat to the woman, and she slams the door. He comes back and mounts his horse.

Suddenly gunfire explodes from the barn. Your horse rears and runs. One of the guards falls to the ground.

You get control of your horse and gallop back to the farmhouse. Jumping off your horse, you race to the injured guard. He's already dead.

Two men stumble out of the barn. You see that Reeves is pushing them forward.

"The wagon's out back," Reeves says. "Load them up."

Then Reeves turns angrily to you. "You ignored your gut feeling that something was wrong, didn't you?"

How could he know? You hang your head and nod shamefully.

"If something doesn't seem right, it probably ain't," he says.

"It won't happen again," you promise.

"Better not, or you'll find yourself dead," Reeves warns.

Reeves orders you and the rest of the posse to bury your companion. As you scrape the hard dirt with a shovel, you feel miserable about what happened. Next time, you'll do better.

THE END

To follow another path, turn to page 9.
To read the conclusion, turn to page 101.

This is a dangerous situation that might get worse. "Okay, boys, let's go," you say. "You're all arrested."

"For what?" one yells.

"Disturbing the peace," you reply in an even voice as you draw your weapon. The cowboys don't move. "Come on," you urge. "I'm not kidding. Put your guns down and take a step back."

The men bend down to put their guns on the ground. As you reach to pick them up, one of the cowboys grabs his gun and fires. A searing hot pain hits you in the stomach, and you crumple to the muddy ground. You don't see the cowboys running away or the crowd that gathers around as you die.

THE END

To follow another path, turn to page 9.
To read the conclusion, turn to page 101.

Deputy marshals were in charge of keeping the peace.

Before the trail boss knows what's happening, you grab his gun away from him. The cowboys stare at you for a moment and then burst out laughing.

"He got you good!" they yell at their boss. "Took that right out of your hand!"

The trail boss glares at you. You look calmly back at him.

"I'm sure you were going to pay them what they're due," you say.

"Uh — of course," the man stammers. Quickly he hands each man his pay, never taking his eyes off your gun.

"Good work, deputy!" the cowboys say as the trail boss dashes away. "Thanks!"

"Now stay out of trouble," you warn the men as they head downtown. You smile as you watch them go. You're sure you'll see them — or others just like them — again in your years to come as a deputy marshal.

THE END

To follow another path, turn to page 9.
To read the conclusion, turn to page 101.

If you don't shoot him, he'll shoot you. You open fire, but you aim low. With a scream, the man falls and clutches his leg. You walk up to him slowly, your gun still pointed at him. You recognize his description from the warrant. He's the criminal you've been looking for. If he doesn't bleed to death, he'll be going back to Fort Smith with you.

You are too focused on the injured man to notice the farmer creeping up behind you. The last thing you hear in your life is the blast from a rifle as you're shot in the back.

THE END

To follow another path, turn to page 9.
To read the conclusion, turn to page 101.

You don't know if the man is the farmer or the outlaw. Besides, there could be someone hiding in the stacks of hay. You carefully creep up the stairs and hide behind several hay bales, waiting to see what happens.

Sure enough, a second man emerges from the shadows of the hayloft and joins the first man. From his rough clothing, you suspect the second man is the farmer. They say something to each other, and then they lower their weapons. You imagine that they think they've won.

"Hands up! You're under arrest by the U.S. marshal!" you yell, pointing both of your pistols at them. "Drop your weapons!"

Turn the page.

They drop their rifles and slowly turn around. Reeves climbs the ladder and joins you.

"Good work, deputy," he says. "This is the criminal we've been looking for and his helper." You lead the men down the ladder. "Both of these men will be tried by Judge Parker for their crimes."

"Judge Parker?" the farmer asks as they're loaded into the wagon. "Hanging Judge Parker?"

Reeves grins. "That's the one," he says with a chuckle. The men look terrified.

It's a 10-day ride back to Fort Smith, and you're not looking forward to taking care of these two criminals. But you know that they will get a fair trial when you return.

Criminals received a fair trail in Judge Parker's courtroom.

THE END

To follow another path, turn to page 9.
To read the conclusion, turn to page 101.

People rushed to Deadwood in Dakota Territory to search for fortune.

CHAPTER 4

In Search of Fortune

Gold! No other word fills your heart with more excitement. It's 1876. Word has reached your town in Illinois that gold was discovered a couple of years ago in the Black Hills of the Dakota Territory. You know you have to go. Ever since you returned from the Civil War in 1865, you've been working as a blacksmith. Now it's time for some adventure.

Before you know it, you're heading toward Dakota Territory. After weeks of travel, you finally arrive in a mining town called Deadwood. In front of you stretches a sea of dirty tents and half-built structures clinging to the sides of a deep gulch.

Turn the page.

The place is swarming with people, mostly men, who have come here to strike it rich. The air is filled with the ringing of hammers, the thunder of wagons, and the stench of horse droppings. You're not sure where to go first.

You wander through the crowd until you find a tent with a hand-painted sign reading "Cricket Saloon." It's loud and smelly inside the tent, but you don't care.

"New in town?" the bartender asks as he hands you a drink.

"I'm here to strike it rich!" you tell him.

The man laughs. "Well, you won't do it in the gold mines. That's for sure," he says. "Your best bet is to make your money at the gambling table."

"Well, if gambling is so good, why are you here serving drinks?" you ask.

The man glares at you. Then he bursts out laughing. "Good question!" he says, holding out his hand. "I'm Al Swearengen. Gambling and gold mining are for fools. One day, I'll have a grand theater in this town. I'm going to call it the Gem. I'll be the richest man in Deadwood without gambling away a penny."

The person beside you chuckles. "You tell him, Al!" You're shocked to hear a woman's voice, and you turn. A tall woman in man's clothing is standing beside you.

"This here's Calamity Jane," Al says. "Watch out — she's the best shot in Deadwood. She claims she's been a scout for General Custer and rode with the Pony Express. Nothing scares her, believe me."

Turn the page.

Historians believe Calamity Jane's real name was Martha Jane Canary.

You nervously introduce yourself. Calamity Jane nods, then turns to Al. "You seen Wild Bill anywhere?" she asks.

"He's gambling at Saloon 10, I'd expect," Al replies.

"I'll try there," Jane says. "Good to meet you," she says to you as she strides out.

You never thought about gambling. Maybe you could strike it rich at the gaming tables.

➤ To stick with your plan and try mining, go to page 75.

➤ To try your hand at gambling, turn to page 77.

"I think I'll stick to mining," you say with a smile.

Al shakes his head. "Your loss," he says. "But good luck, all the same."

What a friendly man, you think.

It's time to buy supplies. You wander around until you see two men selling tools off the back of a wagon.

"Here you go," one of the men says as you buy a shovel, a pick, and some other tools. "We just got to Deadwood today. I'm Seth Bullock. My partner there is Sol Star. We're here to start a business. We're going to buy a piece of land here in town and build a hardware store. Who knows? We might even get rich!"

"Good luck to all of us then," you say, thinking of the gold you hope to find.

Turn the page.

As you load your horse with supplies, your excitement grows. You make your way out of town toward the mining areas. Hundreds of men are already here, digging and panning for gold all along Whitewood Creek. Finally you find a promising place along the bend of the creek, away from the other miners. You set up camp and get to work.

Weeks go by as you pan for gold. It is boring, backbreaking work. For hours, you scoop water and gravel into a shallow pan and swirl it around. You finally find a small gold nugget, but it's not worth very much. Your excitement is long gone. You wonder why you came here in the first place. Maybe it's time to pack up and go home.

→ To keep trying a little longer, turn to page **80**.

→ To quit mining, turn to page **94**.

Saloons provided a major source of entertainment in the West.

Mining does sound like a lot of work. Getting rich at the gambling tables sounds far more exciting.

"Where's the best place to go?" you ask.

"Saloon 10," Al says. That afternoon you head to Saloon 10. You're surprised to find it crowded this time of day. Hazy blue smoke hangs in the air. Several cowboys lean against the long oak bar. A lively game of cards is going on in the corner. When one man finally leaves, you sit down at the card table.

Turn the page.

"What's your name, stranger?" a large man at the table asks. "I'm Hickok. Some call me Wild Bill."

Wild Bill Hickok! You've heard stories about this famous Wild West gunslinger. He's been a Union army scout, a professional gambler, and even a lawman. You had no idea he was in Deadwood. He must have been the man Calamity Jane was looking for! Beating him at cards might not be that simple, you think uneasily as he deals the cards.

As the night wears on, you manage to hold your own. One man at the table isn't having any luck, though. Jack McCall, who is sitting beside you, is drinking heavily and losing hand after hand. Finally he throws down his cards in a fury.

"Calm down, Jack," Wild Bill says kindly. He hands McCall some money. "Here, take this and get something to eat." McCall glares at Wild Bill, but grabs the money and leaves. Soon after, Wild Bill stands up. "Good to meet you," he says as he leaves. "Come play with us again tomorrow."

It might be time for you to leave too. You don't want to lose the money you've won.

→ To stay for one more hand, turn to page **82**.

→ To call it a night, turn to page **84**.

You still have a little hope of striking it rich. One morning, you wake early and take a walk along the bank. The light from the rising sun makes the water sparkle. But wait — there is another sparkle in the water! You reach down, your heart pounding. Sure enough, it's a gold nugget! Fighting the urge to yell, you quietly look around, but you don't see any more gold. Immediately you move your camp downstream to where you found the nugget.

Just as you finish unpacking your belongings, two rough-looking men appear.

"What do you think you're doing?" they growl. "This is our claim."

You're surprised. You didn't see a camp around here.

Panning for gold was hard work, and few people actually struck it rich.

➤ To pack up and leave, turn to page **94**.

➤ To fight for the spot, turn to page **96**.

One more hand, you decide. To your shock, you are dealt four aces! You don't show any emotion as you bet everything. The pile of money on the table grows as the other players bet as well. When you win the hand, everyone groans. Happily, you put the money in your pocket.

You get up to leave. "Hey, you can't go," one man says. "I want to win my money back!"

"I'll be back tomorrow," you say. As you head out, you feel rough hands pulling you back. You spin around and draw your gun.

"Take your hands off me!" you say loudly.

"You cheated!" the drunken man yells as he sways back and forth, fumbling for his pistol.

➻ *To try to disarm the man, go to page* **83**.

➻ *To shoot him, turn to page* **86**.

"Wait," you say in your most charming voice. The drunken man hesitates. In a flash, you knock the gun from his hand. Two of the man's friends grab him by the arms and carry him out. You pick up the man's gun and hand it to the bartender.

"See that he gets this back, will you?" you say.

The bartender nods. You turn and leave. You've had enough excitement for one night.

Turn the page.

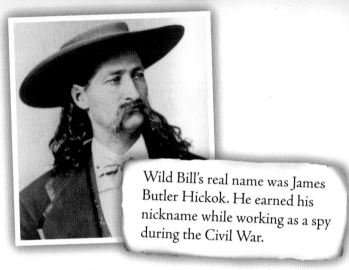

Wild Bill's real name was James Butler Hickok. He earned his nickname while working as a spy during the Civil War.

The next afternoon you make your way back to Saloon 10. Wild Bill isn't there, but several men are already at a table. You smile and take a seat with them. Soon Wild Bill arrives and stands beside the table. He has a troubled look on his face.

"Aren't you going to join us?" you ask. You wave to an empty seat. "There's a place right here for you."

"If I sit in this chair, my back will be to the door," Wild Bill says. "I never sit with my back to the door. It's too dangerous."

"Oh, it's all right," you say. "What's going to happen, anyway?"

"Maybe you're right," Wild Bill says. He looks over his shoulder at the door as he sits in the chair. Soon you're all paying attention to the card game. Your luck from last night seems to be holding. You win a few hands, and a small pile of coins sits in front of you.

After some time, you get up and stretch. "I'm going to take a break," you say. "I'll be back soon."

"Oh, stay for another hand," Wild Bill urges.

➤ To stay for another hand, turn to page **88**.

➤ To take a break outside, turn to page **89**.

No drunken miner is going to get the better of you, you think as you pull the trigger. With a groan, the man falls to the ground, dead. Instantly you're surrounded by several men who point their guns at you.

"It was self-defense!" you cry, holding up your hands. "You saw him. He was going for his gun!"

The men lower their guns. "He's right," one mutters. "Ned was a fool to threaten you."

Slowly the crowd melts away, and you breathe a sigh of relief. That was close. Too close. You didn't realize how dangerous a game of cards could be. Maybe the life of a gambler in Deadwood isn't such a good idea after all. You return to the hotel safely, already planning to leave. It's time to head back to Illinois.

Many men spent their free time at the gambling tables. Fights often broke out when they lost their money.

THE END

To follow another path, turn to page 9.
To read the conclusion, turn to page 101.

"All right, one more," you agree and sit back down. The cards are dealt. As you're looking at your cards, you see a figure walk up behind Wild Bill.

"Hey, McCall," you say. "Come to play with us?"

Jack McCall doesn't answer. Instead, he raises his gun. "Take that!" he cries and pulls the trigger. Wild Bill slumps to the table, a bullet through his head. The cards he is holding fly onto the floor — two eights, two aces, and another one you can't see.

The room erupts in shouts. What do you do?

⟶ *To stay in the saloon with Wild Bill, turn to page* **91**.

⟶ *To chase McCall, turn to page* **92**.

Some historians believe this is the only existing picture of Jack McCall.

"Nah, play a hand without me," you say. "I'll be back in a bit." You walk out into the street. It's late afternoon, and the sun is warm. As you stretch, Jack McCall strides past you.

Turn the page.

"You're missing a good game," you say to him as he passes. He ignores you and walks into the saloon. A moment later, you hear a gunshot, then screams. McCall comes running out of the saloon.

"What's going on?" you yell after him. McCall tries to mount a horse tied out front, but the saddle is loose and he falls off. Looking around wildly, he runs down the street.

A man runs out of the saloon and shouts, "McCall shot Wild Bill!"

➤ If you run inside the saloon to help Wild Bill, go to page **91**.

➤ If you go after McCall, turn to page **92**.

You rush to Wild Bill, but it's clear that he's dead. Blood is everywhere. From somewhere outside a woman screams, "Wild Bill is shot! Wild Bill is shot!"

It's not long before McCall is caught and brought back to town. "He killed my brother," McCall cries as he's led to the jail. "Wild Bill killed my brother, so I had to kill him!"

Several of Wild Bill's friends take his body away. You watch them go, still not quite believing what just happened.

Turn to page 98.

"Let's get him, boys!" you yell. A crowd follows you as you chase McCall through town. You finally find him hiding in a butcher shop. The crowd takes McCall back to the saloon and hands him over to a group of deputies. They roughly drag him to the jail.

When you go into the saloon, Wild Bill's friends are already there. Calamity Jane is crying in a corner. Carefully the men carry Wild Bill's body out as a group of townspeople follows behind. You can't believe what has happened. Then the men disappear into a house with Wild Bill's body.

WILD BILL

J B HICKOK
DIED aug 2 1876
BY PISTOL SHOT
AGED 37 years
CUSTER
WAS LONELY
WITHOUT HIM

ERECTED BY
J H RIORDAN
OF N.Y 1891

WILD
BILL

A monument stands over
Wild Bill's grave. People
can visit the grave today in
Deadwood, South Dakota.

Turn to page 98.

Even though you've found some gold, you decide mining is not worth the effort. You've had enough. Packing up your belongings, you make your way back to Deadwood. You've got enough gold to get you back to Illinois. But you're not quite ready to leave yet.

As you wander through Deadwood, you marvel again at the bustle and excitement in town. Buildings are going up so fast that the town looks different every day. Everywhere you go, there is a new business. Stores sell everything from mining supplies to peanuts. Saloons and dance halls crowd between general stores, drugstores, hotels, and even law offices.

Suddenly an idea grips you. You could open a blacksmith shop in Deadwood!

By the end of 1876, Deadwood was a booming community.

With your gold money, you buy a small piece of land at one end of town and build a smithy. Before you know it, you have more business than you can handle. It's not long before you're one of the wealthiest businessmen in town. It's not exactly how you imagined striking it rich, but it's fine with you.

THE END

To follow another path, turn to page 9.
To read the conclusion, turn to page 101.

"There's no camp around here. I think you're lying," you say, drawing your guns and firing at the two men.

They yell, both drawing their guns as they jump away. You have just enough time to scramble to the back of your tent before the two start shooting. You duck as several bullets tear through your tent, barely missing you. You peek around the tent and aim for the closest man, who is crouched behind a tree. You fire and miss. Another gun blast hits the ground beside you, blasting dirt into the air.

You're not giving up this spot without a fight. The man by the tree stands up. You fire, knocking him down. Quickly you crawl around the tent to find the other man.

As you do, two shots come from the creek. One slams into your stomach. Blood spurts everywhere. The hard gold nugget in your pocket feels cold as you sink to the ground, dying.

THE END

To follow another path, turn to page 9.
To read the conclusion, turn to page 101.

The next morning, a hasty trial is held. The only witness called is Jack McCall himself. The jury listens to McCall's claim that Wild Bill killed his brother. To your astonishment, the jury returns a verdict of not guilty. The courtroom is stunned. Even McCall looks shocked. Before anyone has time to react, the judge tells McCall to get out of town and never come back.

"If Wild Bill did kill his brother, then McCall was justified," say some.

"Jack McCall is a low-down, cold-blooded murderer!" others say. You agree.

You really didn't believe how dangerous and lawless the West was until now. You've decided Deadwood is too wild for you. Your old life as a blacksmith in Illinois is looking pretty good. The next day you pack your belongings and head home.

THE END

To follow another path, turn to page 9.
To read the conclusion, turn to page 101.

Stories of outlaws robbing trains filled books and newspapers.

CHAPTER 5

Taming the Wild West

By the 1890s, the era of the Wild West was almost over. The last great American Indian Plains tribes were defeated. The huge buffalo herds that once blackened the prairie were gone. Most areas of the West were settled. Towns and villages rose where wilderness once stretched for miles. In 1893, historian Frederick Jackson Turner wrote the American frontier was closed.

The Wild West had been known as a place of adventure and danger. Books filled with thrilling stories of train robberies and murders spread those ideas.

Newspapers published stories of how Jesse James robbed from the rich and gave to the poor. Stories painted Billy the Kid as a fearless teenage gunslinger. Reports told of the Wild Bunch, led by Butch Cassidy and the Sundance Kid, and their adventures robbing trains and banks.

But the truth of the Wild West was much different than the exciting stories. In fact, the stories were rarely true. There is no record of Jesse ever sharing his loot with anyone but himself. Billy the Kid killed innocent people, stole cattle, and was eventually killed himself. All the members of the Wild Bunch were either killed or put in prison.

Wyatt Earp is a legend of the Wild West.

Lawmen in the West worked hard to control the lawlessness, but it wasn't easy. Judge Isaac Parker got the name "Hanging Judge" because 79 criminals were hanged during his career in Fort Smith. Pat Garrett is known as the sheriff who finally killed Billy the Kid. Wyatt Earp became a legend when he led a gunfight against thieves in Tombstone, Arizona.

The legends of the Wild West weren't always men. Some rough-and-tumble women also became famous. Calamity Jane may have been an army scout and a Pony Express rider. Belle Starr was another legendary Wild West woman. Along with her husband, Sam Starr, Belle started an outlaw gang. Together they stole cattle and horses until they were caught in 1882.

These women were unusual in the West, though. Most Wild West women lived quieter lives as wives and mothers. Many women had businesses, such as restaurants or shops, in towns throughout the West. Others worked at less respectable jobs, such as saloon girls and dance hall girls.

Most women in the West worked hard running their farms and caring for their families.

By the end of the 1800s, the romance of the Wild West, and the people who lived it, were almost gone. Things changed as more people moved west. People wanted to be safe in the towns they settled. Towns hired sheriffs and other lawmen. Outlaws were killed or put in jail. But the adventure, excitement, and danger of the Wild West lives on in the stories that have been passed down through the years.

Time Line

1860 — Abraham Lincoln is elected president of the United States.

1861–1865 — The Civil War is fought between the southern Confederate and northern Union armies.

1866 — The first daytime robbery of a U.S. bank is committed in Liberty, Missouri. It has never been proven, but many believe Jesse and Frank James led the robbery.

1867 — The first cattle drive from Texas to Kansas occurs on the Chisholm Trail.

1870 — The town of Wichita, Kansas, is founded.

1873 — The James gang pulls its first train robbery.

 1874 — Gold is discovered in the Black Hills of the Dakota Territory.

1875 — The town of Deadwood is founded in the Black Hills.

Judge Isaac Parker holds his first court in Fort Smith, Arkansas.

The U.S. government offers to buy the Black Hills. The Lakota Indians refuse the offer.

1876 — On June 25, the Lakota Indians defeat George Armstrong Custer's soldiers at the Battle of Little Bighorn in Montana Territory.

On August 2, Jack McCall murders Wild Bill Hickok.

On September 7, the James-Younger gang attempts to rob a bank in Northfield, Minnesota.

1879 — The town of Deadwood burns to the ground and is rebuilt.

1882 — Bob Ford assassinates Jesse James.

1889 — Dakota Territory is admitted to the Union as the states of North and South Dakota.

1893 — Frederick Jackson Turner declares that the western frontier is closed.

OTHER PATHS TO EXPLORE

In this book, you've seen how the events experienced by people in the Wild West look different from three points of view.

Perspectives on history are as varied as the people who lived it. You can explore other paths on your own to learn more about what happened. Seeing history from many points of view is an important part of understanding it.

Here are some ideas for other Wild West points of view to explore:

- ✦ Cowboys traveled many miles over empty prairies. What was it like for these men when they arrived at a town and had time to rest and money to spend?

- ✦ Many citizens of towns like Wichita feared the rowdy cowboys who came with the cattle drives. If you had lived in Wichita at that time, how would you have felt?

- ✦ Outlaws risked their lives to steal fortunes. What would life be like for a person on the run from the law?

READ MORE

Bard, Jessica. *Lawmen and Outlaws: The Wild, Wild West.* New York: Children's Press, 2005.

Green, Carl R., and William R. Sanford. *Jesse James.* Berkeley Heights, N.J.: Enslow, 2009.

Raum, Elizabeth. *Wild West Legends.* Chicago: Raintree, 2008.

Robinson, J. Dennis. *Jesse James: Legendary Rebel and Outlaw.* Minneapolis: Compass Point Books, 2007.

INTERNET SITES

FactHound offers a safe, fun way to find educator-approved Internet sites related to this book.

Here's what you do:

    1. Visit *www.facthound.com*
    2. Choose your grade level.
    3. Begin your search.

This book's ID number is 9781429623421.

FactHound will fetch the best sites for you!

GLOSSARY

claim (KLAYM) — a piece of land for which a miner has declared a right to occupy and search for valuable minerals

deputy (DEP-yuh-tee) — a person appointed as an assistant law enforcement officer

gallows (GAL-ohz) — a wooden frame used for hanging criminals

gulch (GUHLCH) — a deep valley that fills with water when it rains

gully (GUHL-ee) — a long, narrow ravine or ditch

gunslinger (GUN-sling-uhr) — a person noted for his or her speed and skill in handling a gun

marshal (MAR-shul) — an officer of a federal court who has duties similar to those of a sheriff

posse (POSS-ee) — a group of people gathered together to help catch a criminal

saloon (suh-LOON) — a bar where people can buy and drink alcoholic beverages

sharpshooter (SHARP-shoo-tuhr) — a person who shoots a gun with high accuracy

BIBLIOGRAPHY

Adams Museum and House
http://www.adamsmuseumandhouse.org

Drago, Harry Sinclair. *The Legend Makers: Tales of the Old-Time Peace Officers and Desperadoes of the Frontier.* New York: Dodd, Mead, 1975.

Fort Smith National Historical Site
http://www.nps.gov/fosm/historyculture/outlaws.htm

Horan, James D. *The Authentic Wild West: The Gunfighters.* New York: Crown Publishers, 1976.

Horan, James D. *The Authentic Wild West: The Outlaws.* New York: Crown Publishers, 1977.

Library of Congress
http://memory.loc.gov/learn/features/timeline/riseind/west/west.html

Northfield Historical Society
http://www.northfieldhistory.org

O'Neal, Bill, James A. Crutchfield, and Dale L. Walker. *The Wild West.* Lincolnwood, Ill.: Publications International, 2001.

Parker, Watson. *Deadwood: The Golden Years.* Lincoln, Neb.: University of Nebraska Press, 1981.

INDEX